Make Money Writing:
a freelancer's intensive

companion booklet to the video series

by

Terry Persun

To a brighter future for everyone

Table of Contents

Chapter 1:
What Do You Know?

My YouTube course, *Make Money Writing: a freelancer's intensive*, was produced because so many people have taken my class at writers' conferences and wanted to repeat it. I thought that it would be easier to create a dozen short videos or so than to continually offer the class at a hotel or conference. This way, interested viewers don't have to pay for the course (I'll monetize it using YouTube ads). This means that I'll collect a smaller amount, but it will also be available to larger numbers of people. You can get to my YouTube channel here: https://www.youtube.com/channel/UCJ-kAsxmPR0Wb39PT996h4Q

The course explains the key elements of how to make a living while freelance writing. This is something I've been doing for over fifteen years. I've actually been freelance writing (fiction, nonfiction, and poetry) for over thirty, but had a regular job for half that time. Many of those years, I was freelancing part time, while working as the Editor-in-Chief of several commercial and business-to-business magazines. So, I've been on both sides of the desk: acquisitions as an editor, and pitching as a freelancer. I know this business well.

Because of the potential income that you can make, I've focused this course on writing nonfiction pieces rather than fiction or poetry. Nonetheless, all the suggestions and rules apply to fiction and poetry as well as nonfiction. And, I do make part of my income through fiction writing, so it's very relevant. And, who knows, we're all different. Perhaps you'll find that writing fiction is easier and pays better for you. Either way, this course will provide you with all the relevant details you'll need.

This first part is fairly simple, but very important. It is going to be the basis of a lot of your future work, so don't pass this by or select not to do the necessary work involved. So, welcome, and let's get started. Get out your laptop or notebook and pen, because this first part is all about an exploration of you. Trust me, though, it'll be easy.

The first thing I want you to do is to make a list of the actual jobs you've had throughout your life. Start with jobs you got paid for directly, like accountant, engineer, or oceanographer. Most people have had several jobs and often more than one career throughout their lives, so go back to the beginning. I want you to cover everything.

For example, when I was very young, I helped tear down and salvage the materials from buildings that were condemned. I also worked as a gas station attendant, a cook at a fast food chain, major appliance repair (including refrigeration), an airborne electronics repairman, an electronics technician, a hardware electronics engineer, a technical writer, an editor, a marketing assistant, a marketing director, a sales manager, and the operations manager for a factory. I know, I've been around. So, make your own list and set it aside.

Now make a list of the jobs you've performed and know something about that you haven't been paid for. We all do a lot of things around the house and for our friends and neighbors, so think back over your life for a list. Again, my example might include being a husband and father, a minor mechanic (around the house and with our vehicles), electrician (around the house at home and for friends), major appliance repairman (for our own appliances as well as friends'), gardener, grocery shopper...you get the picture. Once again, set that list aside.

Your third list is to include your hobbies. When I'm not doing anything else, I enjoy studying books on writing, reading all sorts of things, riding horses, hiking along the beach or in the mountains, painting, and building things out of wood (from bookshelves to chick coops).

Your final list is of things you are interested in. Like the other lists, this one could include anything from previous lists (go ahead and put things down on two or three different lists). You may have worked in a field where you are still engaged as a hobby. Or this final list could include items not yet included, such as astrology, history, UFOs, bigfoot, and building rock walls.

Now it's time to sit down with your four list and prioritize your entries in two lists, one that indicates subjects you know the most about, and feel confident that you have something to offer those who know less about it than you. Start with the fields you are most proficient in and work down to those you are least proficient in. Your second list should be prioritized from most interested to least interested. This list includes things you may have written down as a hobby or something you'd just like to know more about and would have fun researching.

Here is a list indicating that there are over 2500 magazines available to write for. Since this is not a complete list, I'd venture to day there are probably three to five times more than this. And, this is a list of print magazines. There are an equal or triple number of online magazines either affiliated with these print magazines or stand-alones.

African-American (26)
  Culture (19)
  Men (1)
  Women (6)

Animals & Pets (52)
  Birds (6)
  Cat (6)
  Dog (15)
  Fish/Aquariums (3)
  Horses (15)
  Pets (7)

Art & Antiques (65)
  Antiques (8)
  Art (47)

Dance (5)
Painting (4)
Theatre Arts (1)

Auto (119)
  Auto News (20)
  Auto Repair/Acc (6)
  Buying & Selling (9)
  Classic Cars (10)
  Hot Rods (11)
  Motocross (7)
  Motorcycle (16)
  Mustangs/Fords (5)
  Offroad Vehicle (11)
  Sports Cars (13)
  Motorhomes (3)

Trucks (8)
Boat (25)
Boat Enthusiast (8)
Canoes/Kayaks (3)
Power Boats (6)
Sail Boats (4)
Yachts (4)

Books & Literature (56)
African-American (1)
Book Reviews (7)
Christian (20)
Fiction (16)
Judaism (5)
Science Fiction (7)

Business & Finance (73)
Mgmt/Exec (10)
Business/Finance 17
Foreign Business 10
Local Business (15)
Personal Finance 11
Small Business 10

Collectibles (64)
Sports Cars (2)
Coin Collecting (8)
Comics (40)
Sports Collectibles 3
Stamp Collector (3)
Toys (4)
Trading Cards (2)
Baseball (1)
Football (1)

Computers/Electronic 52
Audio & Video (11)
Computer Intersts 20
Programming (10)
Video Games (11)

Cooking & Food (59)

Baking (3)
Beer (5)
Cooking Guide (37)
Gourmet Food (6)
Wine (8)

Crafts & Hobbies (150)
Painting (1)
Small Business (1)
Airplanes & Flying (14)
Dolls/Dollhouses (6)
Jewelry (13)
Knitt/Crochet (15
Model Cars/planes 8
Photography (14)
Projects How To (27)
Quilting (12)
Railroad & Trains 10
Sewing (8)
Woodworking (13)
Writing (8)

Education (11)
Education Admin (6)
Musical Education 3
Public Education (2)

Entertainment (99)
Movies & Cinema 14
Music (47)
Pop Culture (19)
Tabloid (8)
Television (11)

Financial Investment (7)
Kiplinger (5)
Morningstar (2)

Fishing & Hunting (43)
Fishing (23)
Hunting (20)

Health & Science (84)
   Diabetes (3)
   Diet & Nutrition 11
   Medical (33)
   Natural Health (13)
   Science (20)
   Yoga & Pilates (4)

Hispanic (28)
   Hispanic Culture 13
   En Espanol (15)

History (43)
   Science (1)
   American History 21
   Military History (14)
   World History (7)

Home & Garden (123)
   Antiques (1)
   Science (1)
   Country Living (6)
   Decorate/Design 42
   Farm/Ranch Living 9
   Fine Living (25)
   Gardening (11)
   Home Improvemnt 6
   Local Home/Gard 21
   Home Building (1)

Kids & Teens (84)
   Beginng Readers 20
   Children 6-12 (33)
   Just for Girls (12)
   Teen (19)

Lifestyle Interests (103)
   Knitt/Crochet 1
   Pop Culture (2)
   Science (1)
   Yoga & Pilates (1)
   Home Improvemnt 1

Astrology (3)
Cards & Gambling 5
Career (6)
Environmental (6)
Gay & Lesbian (4)
Religion/Spiritual 27
Senior/Retirement 3
World Culture (40)
Running (1)

Local Lifestyle (184)
   En Espanol (1)
   World Culture (1)
   Mid-Atlantic (19)
   Midwest (38)
   New England (38)
   Pacific Coast (22)
   South-Central (5)
   Southeast (38)
   Southwest (16)
   West (6)

Men's (38)
   Cigars (3)
   Men's Health (10)
   Mens Lifestyle (25)

News (44)
   Judaism (1)
   Economics (12)
   General News (5)
   International News 6
   Political News (20)

Outdoors (84)
   Horses (1)
   West (1)
   Bow & Arrow (5)
   Guns & Knives (24)
   Local Outdoors (35)
   Parks & Wildlife (4)
   Recreation (12)

Parenting & Family (38)
  Family (31)
  Motherhood (7)

Professional/Industry 374
  Education Admin (2)
  Elementary Edu (4)
  Public Education (4)
  Medical (4)
  Advertising/Media 8
  Architect/Design 14
  Banking/Credit (7)
  Business Tech (9)
  Commercial Aviation 3
  Construction (4)
  Design (4)
  Entertainmnt/Music 5
  Farming (5)
  Food Service (1)
  Government (57)
  Home Building (2)
  House Plans (1)
  HR/Employment 15
  Industrial (8)
  Manufacturing (3)
  Medicine/Biotech 22
  Military (3)
  Mortgage Industry 5
  News Journalism (3)
  Finance (5)
  Retail/Wholesale (6)
  Sales/Marketing (2)
  Stock Broker (4)

Puzzles & Games (69)
  Crosswords (23)
  Puzzles (20)
  Word Search (26)

Sports (161)
  Baseball (5)
  Basketball (6)

Bicycling (11)
Boxing/Wrestling (2)
Alternative 35
Football (13)
Golf (20)
Racing (8)
Running (4)
Skateboarding (6)
Skiing/Snowboard 15
Soccer (6)
Sporting News (30)

Sports - College (74)
  ACC (11)
  Big East (9)
  Big 10 (12)
  Big 12 (12)
  Mid-Major (4)
  Pac 10 (5)
  SEC (21)

Travel & Vacations (45)
  World Culture (1)
  General Travel (12)
  Internat'l Travel (23)
  Island & Resorts (8)

Women's (130)
  Hispanic Culture (1)
  Family (1)
  Fashion & Style (62)
  Love & Romance 13
  Wedding (9)
  Women's Health 13
  Womens Lifestyle 31

Notice in the list how many magazines are available in each category, then consider what types of articles each might need. For example, a craft and hobby magazine might print articles on a wide variety of hobbies and crafts, but also might require pieces beyond that narrow label, such as general articles on how to run a business, on how to protect yourself legally, on being more creative, on hiring help, or on how to effectively select which shows and fairs suit your interest.

I want you to match your lists to the magazines on this list. Consider your expertise in any one field and how it might cross over to magazines in other fields, and how much fun crossing over with an article might be. For example, say you worked as an accountant for a mechanics shop. The same skills you honed there are transferable to almost any other business. And if you are particularly interested in history, perhaps you could write a piece for a real estate business magazine on some aspect of accounting.

Another example might be that you worked as an engineer, as I did for many years. I can write engineering articles (which I do), but I can also write for a home repair magazine on how to troubleshoot your major appliances before calling the repairman. Or I could write for a garden magazine showing readers how to easily wire in their automatic watering system without having to go through the manual.

So, jot down what magazines you would like to be published

in and produce a list of articles you might be able to write for them. I hope you're beginning to see how many articles need to be written, and how your experience and expertise fit into many of the needs of publishers online and in print.

Chapter 2:
Popular and Trade
Magazines

There is a marked difference between popular or consumer magazines, trade or business-to-business magazines, and scholarly or research magazines. In this section, I'm going to cover a number of criteria about each of these categories that is important for you to know while you're crafting your feature articles. You'll need to understand these differences so that you can focus your article as deeply or generally as required by the particular magazine type. This will also provide you with a general understanding of the types of pieces you might find in each category of magazine.

Although the separations I'll offer may sound as though they are based on common sense, that's not always the case. Many magazines quickly cross from general to specific information depending upon whether the piece has a feature or departmental focus. Ultimately, the best way to understand a magazine is to buy or acquire several copies and read them front to back. Editorial focus as well as writing style may vary within a magazine, and most assuredly from magazine to magazine.

First off let's consider the overall appearance of each category, as well as what type of audience the magazines are hoping to attract:

• Popular magazines often have eye-catching, color covers to attract the general public. The audience for these magazines are often a more general public. Although that general audience can be geared toward men or women, seventeen year olds or retirees, the articles are not meant to be deep explorations. Although, as mentioned, some pieces may go into specific detail, such as comparing skin creams or motor oils.

• Business-to-Business trade magazines offer color covers as well, but typically with an industrial or technical image that is meant to attract members of a specific business or industry. The audience for these magazines are typically controlled, and focus on a particular industry or job function within that industry. Fore example, one magazine may focus on acrospace, but cover all aspects of the industry from mechanics to piloting to seat covers. Another magazine may be focused on engineering and offer articles written for engineers whether they are in aerospace, medical, or industrial automation.

• Scholarly and research magazines often have plain covers, sometimes with color or b/w images, but often no image at all. These magazines focus their articles and other content toward professionals and researchers in the particular category they publish in. These can be medical journals or legal journals.

Primary content for most popular magazines include general interest articles, personality pieces, and news. Many include consumer product sections as well, such as makeup or hiking equipment, or even book reviews. The articles are subject to editorial review for selection. The editors generally accept pieces based on their wide appeal and specific interests of their readers, whether male or female, young or old, as mentioned above.

Content for trade magazines include industrial trends, new products or technologies, case studies, and organizational or association news. These magazines often provide sections on where their readers can acquire free brochures or catalogs on particular companies or particular product categories. Article selection for business-to-business journals also go through an editorial review just as consumer magazines, except that the editors are typically industry experts and are looking for pieces offering more depth and understanding of the particular subject matter.

Scholarly journals include articles on research projects, methodologies, and theory. Written by professionals and researchers, these articles are typically selected by a peer review. The editors of these magazines often provide strict editing services to make sure that the articles are formatted correctly and are understandable to the audience reading them.

The information above provides you with an idea of how much you should know about a particular subject in order to write for each magazine category. Although many freelancers won't be submitting work to scholarly journals, you may be asked (or acquire work) to help an expert write a piece that they'd like to submit to a scholarly journal.

At this point, I want to focus on multi-magazine publishers. In the consumer magazine business, a publisher such as Kalmback (Kalmback.com) produces a number of magazines from Art Jewelry and Bead & Button, to Bird Watching, Scale Auto, and Astronomy. Similarly, trade publisher Penton Media (PentonMedia.com) offers magazines in Agriculture and Business Aviation, as well as Design Engineering, Electrical Systems & Energy, and Wealth Management. Getting into a particular magazine with a publisher that has many magazines may help you pitch to a second magazine from the same publisher. So, you might wish to prioritize companies with multiple magazines closer to the top of your list. Also note that each magazine most likely has more than just their print property. These days magazines also have e-newsletters and a website that they produce. Getting published in their newsletter could put you in line for the next feature online or in their print magazine. I'll discuss this in greater detail in another chapter.

While you're considering which magazines to write for, let me recommend you check out their circulation numbers. Consumer magazines, such as Time, Glamour, and Redbook have millions of issues going into households every month. Many trade journals, although not going to as many locations (perhaps from about 20,000 to several hundred thousand), do go directly to professionals in a particular niche market. Often you can reach 80 percent of one group of professionals by showing up in a single magazine.

To help you decide on where to focus your attention, here is a list of the top 100 magazines when considering circulation only. These are all in the consumer market. Note the publisher names to see where there may be some opportunities for future crossover potential.

Name	Circulation	Publisher
AARP The Magazine	22,274,096	AARP
AARP Bulletin	22,244,820	AARP
Costco Connection	8,654,464	Costco Wholesale
Game Informer	7,629,995	GameStop
Better Homes And Gardens	7,615,581	Meredith
Reader's Digest	4,536,912	The Reader's Digest Assoc.
Good Housekeeping	4,348,641	Hearst Magazines
Family Circle	4,092,525	Meredith
National Geographic	4,029,881	National Geographic Society
People	3,527,541	Time Inc.
Woman's Day	3,311,803	Hearst Magazines
Time	3,289,377	Time Inc.
Taste of Home	3,249,148	The Reader's Digest Assoc.
Ladies' Home Journal	3,225,863	Meredith
Sports Illustrated	3,023,197	Time Inc.
Cosmopolitan	3,015,858	Hearst Magazines
Prevention	2,872,944	Rodale
Southern Living	2,815,523	Time Inc.
AAA Going Places	2,594,402	Auto Club South

AAA Living	2,414,108	Pace Communications
O, The Oprah Magazine	2,386,601	Hearst Magazines
Glamour	2,327,793	Condé Nast Publications
American Rifleman	2,238,735	National Rifle Association
Parents	2,217,788	Meredith
Redbook	2,206,676	Hearst Magazines
American Legion Magazine	2,191,967	American Legion
ESPN The Magazine	2,160,552	ESPN
FamilyFun	2,122,153	Meredith
Martha Stewart Living	2,107,677	Martha S... Living Omnimedia
Smithsonian	2,103,798	Smithsonian Institution
TV Guide	2,032,581	OpenGate Capital
Maxim	2,028,076	Biglari Holdings
Seventeen	2,023,251	Hearst Magazines
American Baby	2,003,627	Meredith
Real Simple	2,001,146	Time Inc.
Us Weekly	1,964,057	Wenner Media
Men's Health	1,818,127	Rodale
InStyle	1,810,539	Time Inc.
Cooking Light	1,809,234	Time Inc.
Entertainment Weekly	1,771,907	Time Inc.
Money	1,728,983	Time Inc.
Every Day with Rachael Ray	1,728,955	Meredith
Food Network Magazine	1,725,723	Hearst Magazines
Guideposts	1,723,194	Guideposts
Golf Digest	1,661,240	Condé Nast Publications
Shape	1,630,741	American Media
Country Living	1,621,448	Hearst Magazines
Women's Health	1,540,105	Rodale
All You	1,528,079	Time Inc.

Bon Appétit	1,521,180	Condé Nast Publications
Fitness	1,501,058	Meredith
Self	1,495,832	Condé Nast Publications
Rolling Stone	1,469,267	Wenner Media
WebMD The Magazine	1,465,718	McMurry/TMG
Golf Magazine	1,418,866	Time Inc.
Health	1,368,701	Time Inc.
Scholastic Parent & Child	1,344,640	Scholastic
More	1,312,365	Meredith
Weight Watchers	1,305,417	Weight Watchers
Popular Science	1,304,017	Bonnier
VFW Magazine	1,285,474	Veterans of Foreign Wars
Ebony	1,280,350	Johnson Publishing Company
Where	1,278,580	Morris Communications
Sunset	1,273,870	Time Inc.
Vogue	1,259,826	Condé Nast Publications
Playboy	1,254,552	Playboy Enterprises
Field & Stream	1,254,256	Bonnier
HGTV Magazine	1,253,555	Hearst Magazines
Popular Mechanics	1,218,589	Hearst Magazines
Car and Driver	1,208,213	Hearst Magazines
Vanity Fair	1,205,229	Condé Nast Publications
The Family Handyman	1,190,242	The Reader's Digest Assoc.
First for Women	1,185,659	Bauer
Allure	1,168,138	Condé Nast Publications
Birds & Blooms	1,165,980	The Reader's Digest Assoc.
Lucky	1,122,251	Condé Nast Publications
Motor Trend	1,118,877	Source Interlink
Elle	1,109,785	Hearst Magazines
Woman's World	1,106,643	Bauer
Boys' Life	1,097,232	Boy Scouts of America

Essence	1,060,774	Time Inc.
The New Yorker	1,055,542	Condé Nast Publications
American Hunter	1,034,033	National Rifle Association
Food & Family	1,024,262	Meredith
Teen Vogue	1,019,853	Condé Nast Publications
Bloomberg Businessweek	989,186	Bloomberg
Travel + Leisure	974,972	Time Inc.
Marie Claire	969,965	Hearst Magazines
Midwest Living	964,966	Meredith
This Old House	963,501	Time Inc.
Food & Wine	947,286	Time Inc.
GQ	938,359	Condé Nast Publications
Scouting	938,145	Boy Scouts of America
Forbes	931,558	Forbes
Reminisce	872,210	The Reader's Digest Assoc.
Traditional Home	864,505	Meredith
Wired	858,818	Condé Nast Publications
Fortune	857,431	Time Inc.
Ser Padres	857,354	Meredith
People StyleWatch	830,465	Time Inc.

Chapter 3:
Anatomy of a Magazine

It's important for any freelance writer to know the components of print magazines, which are often transferable to online magazines, so that they understand how to maneuver in this industry. In this chapter, I'll discuss the important parts of the magazine and why they are important. After we go over the magazine, I'm going to spend a little time running through some of the components of a media kit, too. The media kit offers a wealth of information about the magazine that is valuable while making the decision where you'd like your work to be published.

First off is the cover. Obvious, I know. But what freelancers need to understand is that the cover art most often reflects one of the main features within the magazine. As a writer, you want to eventually write the feature that the editors choose to illustrate on the cover. Everyone wants to have their piece featured on the cover of their favorite magazine. And getting the cover, as they say, is priceless.

A few covers:

The part of the magazine I want to discuss is the table of contents. This is where you get your first glimpse of the types of features a magazine covers. It also supplies you with key information that many freelancers might see, but don't focus on. Notice the section called *Departments* (or *In Every Issue* or *Regulars*). The departments are included in every issue. I point this out because the departments are the places inside the magazine that the editors have the most difficult time filling. The department stories are shorter in length than most features, and therefore not typically what a freelancer is wanting to provide. That means that the editor may have to adapt a longer piece to a department. This information is critical to the understanding that as a freelancer the departments section is most often easier to break into than the features sections. Where most freelancers are looking to write feature material, the departments are where the editors are searching for material.

A few table of contents pages, showing the departments section:

The next part of a magazine is the masthead. Simply put, this is where you find the names of editors. For many trade magazines (like Machine Design) and some consumer magazines, you can easily find out what section of a magazine a particular editor is responsible for. For example, a lot of business-to-business magazines have experts in particular segments of their industries. They may have an electronics component editor, a mechanical components editor, and a motion control editor. Gearing your query or pitch to the right editor can mean the difference between getting published or not.

A few mastheads:

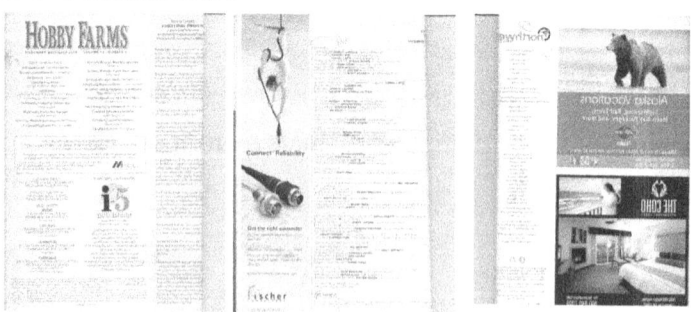

Finally, I like to point out the editorial page. As a freelance writer, it's good to get to know the editor of the magazines you're looking to send articles to. Note what they talk about, what they're interested in, and perhaps find similarities you have with them that you can mention in your pitch. A good way to get the editor to know who you are is to email him or her if you particularly like one of their editorials. If you've written for the magazine through one of their other editors, it's okay to say that you've authored a particular piece, that you've followed the magazine for years, and that you particularly like their editorial for the month. This type of contact can open doors for you to write more pieces in the future.

A few editorial pages:

Now let's go through the parts of a standard media kit. My daughter, Nicole, works for ParentMap, so I decided to use their media kit, which is very well done, as a quick guide to what these promotional pieces have to offer a freelancer.

First of all, early in the media kit, you should find a page that explains all the properties the particular magazine editors are responsible for. For example, the ParentMap franchise offers the print magazine, e-newsletters, annual guides, a standard website (and mobile site), and lecture events. In this list are at leave four potential markets for your articles. Each might be looking for particular content or length, but there is also crossover potential from one to the other.

Besides listing advertising rates for each of the properties, the media kit will have a page or more dedicated to circulation information. Not only will the media kit provide the circulation numbers for each property, it will also break the circulation down into demographics. For example, the 2015 ParentMap Media Kit has an audience of 94% female and 6% male with an average age of between 25 and 44. Their readers also have college degrees (84% of them anyway). Additional information in this section will help any freelance author come up with ideas for articles.

The most important part of the media kit for freelancers, though, is the editorial calendar (or planner), which lets you know what articles the magazine is guaranteeing it will run. The great thing about the editorial calendar is that you can pitch an idea months in advance. By looking over the calendar, you can find potential article ideas that you can research and write...and you know when it's due (about six weeks before the month of publication). Knowing what you're writing ahead of time, and knowing that it's slated for a particular month of publication will help with your budgeting of time, as well as knowing when you might get paid.

You can find the editorial calendars for most magazines online at the magazine site, but you can also contact the sales or editorial offices and they will send you a copy. Make it a point to look over the editorial calendars of the magazines you are hoping to be published in, so you are familiar with what upcoming issues will need.

Chapter 4:
The Five Types of Articles

We've talked about the departments that each magazine has, and that you have to read through them to see what type of material they want for those sections. The departments often have their own look and feel, but some provide full feature material as well. And that's why I'm going to spend time on talking about the main types of articles you can write. There are other ways to approach the writing of feature articles, but these are the most commonly used. Note that the explanations below often overlap depending on the main focus of a certain type of information you include.

The first feature article type is the Informational or Technical piece. How I look at it, these articles are the ones that include very little background information, and quickly go into specific and technical details about a product, a process, a philosophy, or a theory. These articles are the one's you read where the author includes their source materials, along with quotes from experts they may have talked with (or people who were directly involved in the particular topic). These pieces also include back-up research data if applicable. Possible titles for these types of articles might include: "Hardware versus Software: where to start your design" OR "A Short History of Quilting in America".

The second type of feature is the Interview. These features are fairly straight forward, but come in two varieties. The first is a strict interview where it is presented in a question and answer format. The second is where the author discusses the surroundings, the subject on a broader level, and may even add comments concerning history or what others wrote in order to lead the reader through the discussion. This type can also include an interview with just one person or several who are involved in a single subject. These pieces provide an insider's look on a particular subject, or person responsible for the product process, philosophy, or theory. These articles can explore why the interviewee(s) got involved in the focus subject, or questions directly related to the subject itself that explains how the interviewee(s) explored the subject. Possible titles for these types of articles might include: "Software Engineers Discuss Animation Software" OR "How One Writer Creates Characters".

The Application Article or Case Study, as they are sometimes called, focuses on why certain products were used, how they were used, and what differences their use made in the end product. These are sometimes called Solution pieces, too, because they are often written by mentioning a problem, then options for correcting the problem, and then final solutions to the problem and, as a conclusion, why the solution made the product better in the end. Possible titles for these types of articles might include: "Electric Motors Replace Hydraulics for Cleaner Operations"

OR "Automated Pill Counters Help Pharmacists Save Money".

The next type of article is the How-To piece. These features include how to apply, how to use, and how to maintain... type information. They often explain a process or provide information for how to use a product without focusing on the whys. Usually these pieces include steps in order from start to finish. They are the articles written to help non-technical or non-handy people complete tasks, like cleaning silver, building a bookcase, changing the oil on your car, or how to maintain your lawn equipment. Possible titles for these types of articles might include: "How to Maintain Your Older Production Machines" OR "Five Steps to the Perfect Quilt".

Finally, I'll discuss the News stories. These are often short pieces that cover things like mergers, new hires, sales records, etc. These pieces can also cover new product introductions and expanded services being offered. Although they are often short newsy items, these pieces can also extend to article length. For a complicated introduction of some new product or service, it may take more space to cover all the benefits. Possible titles for these types of articles might include: "XYZ Company Buys Competitor" OR "Sales Team Gains New Member" OR "Phone Case Now Comes in Five Colors"

Again, some information found in one of these article types may also be found in another one, and this is how you get to extend your reach as an author with the least amount of additional effort. For example, let's say you talked with a knitting group about some new materials and products that they use, so that you could cover the products in an article. While you're talking with them, you learn that they all came to knitting in a different way. This could easily be expanded into its own article about why people come to knitting, where you interview each of the people in the group. A third article might even come out of this when you find that the person who started the group still ran it. Another article, then might be about that person and why they wanted to create a community around what they loved, or you could write an article about how to start a knitting club in your community.

The idea is always to take advantage of all the information you have available to you. Writing more than one piece from a few short interviews and a little research, can extend your income without extending your time gathering information from a totally new source.

Chapter 5:
Key Article Components

So far, we've talked about what you know and, therefore, what you might write about. We've talked about the different types of magazines, and gone over the different parts of a magazine. Then we advanced to the different types of articles. Now we're going to cover the key components that make up an article.

The first thing I want to cover is the part of the article most often seen and read first: the headline. This is also the part of the article that appears in the table of contents and possibly on the cover. You want this to be good. Short is always better, but when you can't make it short and descriptive, then long is okay. My suggestion is to try to produce headlines that tell the reader what the article is about. Being vague doesn't work here. Using cute phrasing or abstract ideas doesn't attract a reader into a piece, either. Today's readers want to know what they're in for long before they relinquish their time and attention to read through an article. For trade journals, this is even more important because those readers may not have the time to read a whole magazine. They're looking for specific information. Some headings might include: "Measurement Equipment Validates Race Car Components" OR "Laser Sintering Used to Build Electric Motorcycle".

Below the headline, or off to the side, there is often a short sentence or two that adds additional information to the headline to help pull the reader into the article. This is called the deck, it is your hook. But always remember to know who it is you're trying to hook. A deck with general information may not attract someone who is looking for a specific solution to a problem. Similarly, a deck that offers in-depth detail may put off a reader just looking for some general information. The deck will, therefore, reflect what the article will deliver. Some decks might read like this: "Industrial design competitions are reaching out to more engineers than ever before, and with the latest technology, it's easier than ever to produce a physical model." OR "There are a lot of job functions within a company that require access to CAD drawings, but do not required the stringent capabilities of expensive CAD design tools".

Now is the time for the body copy of the article. This is what you've worked so hard to produce, whether it's a case study or in-depth interview with a key person in a particular subject. Note that a typical page in a standard 7x10-inch magazine runs about 600 words with one piece of artwork. I know we covered articles in a previous chapter, but here's some additional information as to what an article might include: At the beginning, include a clear statement of what the article is tackling. After that, you might have a paragraph or more on what to expect from the article (or some background information), and then go into the body of the article, ending in a conclusion or wrap-up.

Always consider including artwork with your written work. Most often this includes anything from drawings or paintings to charts and graphs to photographs and videos (for online articles). When authoring a piece, no matter what the size, artwork can only help you in the selection process. Magazines have multiple ways to catch a reader's attention, and as an author you need to help them explore all the options. And as I mentioned earlier, if your artwork is good enough, it could end up on the cover of the magazine.

Once you've selected artwork to go with your article, include captions. It's always good to let an editor know what a certain piece of artwork is trying to illustrate. It also helps them understand the piece on a different level. Captions should provide new or additional information from the article itself or they become superfluous. Also include credits whenever applicable.

Most articles are written in such a way as to leave room for a deeper understanding of a particular part of the piece. Some readers may not want to go deeper into a subject, but for those who do, the sidebar is the perfect way to give them that information. For a piece where multiple people were interviewed, a sidebar can also focus on a particular person who may have had some unusual input to the overall subject matter. In that case, a sidebar about that input would be relevant. Sidebar information, because of its nature, is often a lot shorter than the article itself. Most are only a few hundred words or so, and take up less than a full page. For long, multi-page articles, though, a sidebar can also stretch for several pages.

The final key I'd like to discuss has little to do with the presentation of the article in print. That key is editing. Because you want to deliver the best piece you possibly can, it's often good to have it edited by someone else. The cleaner your article is when it appears on an editor's desk, the better chance it has to be selected for publication.

Chapter 6:
Starting Your
Freelancing Business

This chapter is focused on getting your business started. For a lot of people, this can be difficult. Many of us have a hard time starting out, so give yourself a break and start out slowly. Remember that getting published is the goal. So any publication credit is valuable, even your work's in-house newsletter. In fact, you might want to start out with a blog. This will, at least, get you writing. I know writers who've started with a blog on a subject they are passionate about and eventually ended up with a book contract, and thousands of followers. So, leave no idea out.

Other avenues for publication include local newspapers from your town and surrounding towns. One publisher often puts out several of the local papers, so once you've been published in one it's easy to get published in the others. Another great starting point are newsletters. Most local groups, whether knitting, gardening, or horseback riding, have a small circulation newsletter that they're always looking to fill with interesting pieces. Organizations offer newsletters as well. Then there are the small local tourist magazines, that are primarily advertising tools, but need articles as filler. From there it's easy to graduate to national newspapers, association newsletters, and larger circulation magazines. Most importantly, don't limit yourself. Search out both print and online venues. If you have written and published in the past, start at the top of the food chain. If an article or departmental piece isn't picked up the first time you send it out, go to the next place on your list.

As you begin to get published, the next thing you'll want to do is create a portfolio. When you're looking to get published in a magazine where you haven't published yet, the editor will most likely ask for samples of other articles you've written, so that he or she can see how well you write, what your style is, and to make sure that you know how to do your research. These samples can take the form of actual tear sheets (or copies) from magazines or a list of links for online pieces. I've even gone so far as to create a multi page PDF that I can send out. Such a PDF can also be formatted to look like a magazine and, through the use of one of the online publishing venues, be turned into a 24 or 36 page magazine that you can mail or hand out. I keep PDFs handy for different industries, but also have a list of links for online appearances, and a spreadsheet for print appearances.

When it comes to initial contact with an editor, I typically look up an editor's name and call them if I have an article already written that I think fits their magazine. This approach, of course, only works after you've been published often enough. For the beginner, I recommend you contact an associate editor or senior editor who handles a special section of the magazine you wish to publish in. In the beginning, calling can be a touch and go situation, so if you haven't been published the particular magazine before, it's advisable to email or snail mail the editor—but do use an editor's name. Blind submissions get far less scrutiny than those aimed at a particular person.

Note that many editors attend trade shows and conferences that correspond to their magazine's interest. There are knitting conferences and shows, wine making conferences, engineering conferences, and anything else you can think of. Find out which magazines are going to attend, make an appointment to meet with an editor if possible, and start to make contact face-to-face. Any way you are able to get to know an editor will help you get started. I've mentioned this before, but as a side note, once you've worked with a magazine, check out if their publishing company has other magazines where you could get published, and then ask if you can use your editor as a reference, or as them to refer you, and possibly make an email introduction.

The next thing is to hand in your best work. I've mentioned this often in these pages, but handing in clean, well-written articles will help you maintain a good reputation among editors. Trust me, they will love you for it.

Finally, there are several ways to make a living freelancing. First off, freelancers can write pieces they want to write, pieces they are interested in and passionate about, then pitch them and sell them to magazines in need of articles. Another way is to work directly with a company that needs articles and releases written about them and their products or services. These pieces you can then pitch to trade or consumer magazines and newspapers. The business pays you to write the piece, so the magazine doesn't have to. This will broaden the number of magazines you can publish in. Many trade publications pay very little or not at all for publication. It's often good to work with editors using both of these methods. If you work for a company, consider producing additional pieces from the same article, including white papers, technical notes, pamphlets or brochures, video scripts, etc.

The important idea to get from this chapter is that you'll want to publish every way and in every venue you can. The more you publish broadly, the better chance you have to continue publishing and getting paid better for it. Stretch your writing to include every type of piece and get published everywhere you can. I still create guest blogs for free, just to stay in the game.

Chapter 7:
Getting Published and
Staying Published

Now is the time to pull everything together and keep the business that you started in the last chapter going forward. This chapter is about keeping your momentum, staying published, maintaining your business for years. There are five basic elements, as mentioned in the title, and the first is the one that will ground you—account for your work.

To account for your work, it's best to set up a production goal. This can be anything from completing a piece a month, a piece a week, or a piece every other day. Be reasonable with yourself and make sure the goal is something you can achieve fairly easily at first. It's better to over produce based on your goal than to never reach your goal, which can be debilitating. I write every day, and have made that my goal so that I don't have to worry about when I finish a piece. As long as I continue to work on it until the end, I'm getting things done.

Part of accounting for your work is keeping more than one article or piece of writing going at the same time. I suggest working on different types of writing, whether fiction and nonfiction or on pieces on different subject matter, such as knitting and engineering. Keeping more than one piece going allows you to continue writing for longer periods of time without getting bored or tired. And, sometimes, the research for one piece can bring up an idea for another one.

Keep your finished work circulating. Don't let any article come back without sending it right back out again. And organize everything: your workload goals, all the pieces you're working on, and where you've sent them and what has been rejected or accepted. Organization is key in keeping your business going and key in accounting for your work. And, finally, tear sheet published piece or keep a list of links, or a spreadsheet of print appearances.

The next thing I want you to do is to conceptualize your whole business as though it were a relationship. This means that your first contact with a magazine is your chance to make a good first impression. Provide editors with clean copy, spell their name correctly on your query letter, and thank them for looking over your work. Even if you are rejected, be kind. I often send back a note in response thanking the editor for his or her time, and letting them know that I am working on other pieces that may be better suited to their needs. You can never be too kind.

Even though you have a relationship with editors and magazines, it is still important to play the field in the sense that sending a particular article out to more than one magazine increases your chances of acceptance. Unless you have a great relationship with an editor who you suspect will take your piece (because they have many times before), send every article to more than one magazine, newsletter, or paper. And, once you do have a good relationship with an editor, don't lower your standards. Continue to give them your best work. After all, you want the relationship to flourish, not to die.

The next thing you want to do is to begin to get to know other freelancers. By creating a community of equals, you have people to talk with about the business. I have more than a few friends who write for a living—everything from fiction and poetry to nonfiction and advertising copy. Many writers are introverts, but it's important to make friends. This also gives you a network to ask for help if you're stuck on a piece, or if you need a person with a particular expertise to look over an article for accuracy. My friends and I often pass our articles and stories back and forth to catch any unfortunate typos.

Stay in touch with your community: write notes, emails, make phone calls. I like to go to coffee with my friends in the business so we can discuss what's going on with certain magazines. These get-togethers are also a good place to share in your successes with one another. A little support can go a long way when most of the time you're sitting behind your computer.

What's important is that you start to live the life of a freelance writer. This is why you started in the first place, so now is the time to bring it full circle. Stay focused on your new job and continue working regularly. You must be self-motivated to make a living as a freelancer. Also, bet out in the public. Go to conferences, talks, and trade shows pertinent to the types of articles you are writing. Meet with editors from magazines where your work could potentially appear. And market yourself as well as your friends, if their work is applicable. I've gotten my friends article placements just because I knew they were working on a particular piece and I happen to meet an editor of a potential magazine for that piece. Both my friend and the editor of the magazine were thankful, and it helped me get published in later magazines.

Finally, and I never want you to forget this part—have fun and play. Yes, you want to love your job, and that won't happen if it all feels like work, work, work. So, create time to just write, whether it's stream of consciousness, journal writing, letter writing, or just complaining. Play with words and ideas you wouldn't normally play with. Do exercises to stretch your writing muscles. Explore everything. Remember, writing is an adventure, treat it as such.

Chapter 8: Applying Nonfiction Rules to Fiction and Poetry

In this last chapter, I want to go over the other chapter information only with a focus on fiction and poetry. Let's remember that typically there are more outlets for nonfiction articles than for fiction, and that most nonfiction outlets pay better. But that doesn't mean that you can't make a living writing fiction. In the least, you can supplement your income with fiction and poetry.

Chapter one is all about knowing who you are and what you know. For fiction, I like to think of it as what do you love? what message do you want to send out to the world? or how would you like to entertain? There are other ways of looking at it, but I think you get where I'm going with this. What you know can help inform your fiction and poetry, but it's not necessarily the only thing you use while writing. Another way to get a fix on what to write is to ask yourself what you read: romance, crime fiction, thrillers, fantasy, science fiction, fiction with an underlying environmental or cultural bent. Answering these questions will help you know where to put your time an energy. Of course, most fiction and poetry writers already have ideas they are passionate about. Spend time there.

By rereading the chapters I reference here, you can apply the idea of fiction and poetry more easily. So when, in chapter two, I talked about the different types of magazines, recognize that there are similar segments in magazines that publish a lot of poetry or fiction. There are university run presses that not only publish a magazine, but often have a book publishing arm. Getting your work published in their magazine may lead to a better chance to have a book accepted by them as well. Other places include what are called small presses and micro presses. There are all sorts of ways to separate these magazines out, but I typically look at circulation (as with other magazines). A lot of small presses have circulations in the thousands, where micro presses may have circulations in the hundreds. This include both online and print magazines. There are still a few traditionally published popular magazines that publish fiction. Magazines like the New Yorker, the Atlantic, and others. I'm sorry that I don't have a list of such magazines. That's because I focus on the university and small press magazines.

In chapter three I discuss the anatomy of a magazine, and this is pretty much the same for any magazine you run into. So, if you are unsure of how to find certain segments of a magazine, chapter three has everything you may need.

This may sound very basic to many readers, but I'm going to include it anyway. Instead of covering basic article types here, I'm going to do a quick run-through of some basic story and

poetry types, if you will. You can also review chapter four if
you'd like. So, what I'm talking about here are genres and/or
formats. The standard designations include long short story (up to
about 7000 words), short story (under 5000 words), flash fiction
(debatable, but normally under 1000 words, some magazines
specify under 500 or fewer), and poetry, both traditional and free
verse of varying lengths. Additionally, you will find book length
poems and short-short poems like Haiku, as well as longer fiction
pieces from novelettes (about 10,000 words), to novellas (from
10,000 to about 45,000), to book length, which is anything over
about 50,000 up to several hundred thousand.

The other meaning of genre includes what I talked about
earlier, which includes romance, thriller, mystery, fantasy,
science fiction, etc. In poetry that might be narrative, reflective,
descriptive, ballad, ode, elegy, and others.

In chapter five I talked about the key article components to help
you understand what an editor is looking for and how best to
present your articles. For that section—only with fiction and
poetry in mind—the best advice might be to learn how to write
a good story or poem. It's important to learn what a character
arc is, what plot points are, and the hero's journey. Learn about
milieu, character, event, and all the other things needed for you
to tell a good story. With poetry, understand line endings, sound,
metaphor, simile, and how all these points cross over into fiction.
There are plenty of books available that teach these things, so
look them up and study your craft. Go to writers' conferences

to meet other writers, agents, and editors. Learn and continue to learn more as your write. That's what's great about being a writer: you never have to stop learning.

Instead of talking about beginning to create a freelance business like I did in chapter six, I think it's important to just think of this as a learning process and to start mailing out your completed stories, poems, or novels. As with article writing, publish anywhere. The smallest pamphlet, which deals with short stories or poetry can add to your publishing credits. So try the most obscure and tiny magazines and online magazines if you're just beginning—or try the best magazines you can find. It doesn't matter at first. Everything counts. Then start creating your portfolio and lists of links or print appearances. Get to know editors, and ask for referrals. And most important of all, hand in clean work, spell-checked and edited.

Applying chapter seven to fiction and poetry is the easiest thing to do. First of all, if you are reading this booklet sequentially, it's probably fresh in your mind. Second of all, getting published and staying published was originally created for my fiction and poetry audience. I actually applied it to nonfiction just because it works all the way around—in fact, for any goal you may have. So, here are the key points once again: account for your work by setting goals, circulating finished work, and staying organized; conceptualize the process as a relationship and make a good impression, respond kindly, and continue to put out good work; create a community of equals, where you can ask for help, stay in touch, and share in your successes; live the life of the writer by staying focused, going to conferences and fairs, and marketing yourself and your work; and finally, have fun – if your career isn't fun, why do it?

Thank you for sticking with this. I know there is a lot of information here. Creating a freelancing business or starting to get published at all is a big step. I suggest you highlight pieces of this booklet and go back and review them. Or, since it's short, reread the whole thing again and again. The most important thing to get out of this is that you can write and begin a career as an author. With more internet sites going up every day, and more magazines, television programs, movies, books, newsletters, and newspapers there is no shortage of the need for great pieces. Be part of it by starting now.

END

About the author

Terry Persun writes in many genres, including historical fiction, mainstream, literary, and science fiction/fantasy. He is a Pushcart nominee. His latest poetry collection is *Sentences*. His novel, *Cathedral of Dreams* is a ForeWord magazine Book of the Year finalist in the science fiction category, and his novel *Sweet Song* won a Silver IPPY Award. His latest literery novel, *Ten Months in Wonderland*, and his latest science fiction novel *Hear No Evil* were both International Book Award finalists.

www.TerryPersun.com

Other works by Terry Persun

Mainstream Novels:
Ten Months in Wonderland
The Perceived Darkness
Wolf's Rite
Giver of Gifts
Deception Creek
The Witness Tree

Science Fiction Novels:
Hear No Evil
Revision 7:DNA
Backyard Aliens
Cathedral of Dreams

Fantasy Series:
Doublesight
Memory Tower
Fugitives
Gargoyle

Historical Novel:
Sweet Song

Detective/Crime Novels:
The NSA Files (a Dan Johnston, Shaman Detective novel)
Mistake in Identity
Man by the Door

Poetry Collections:
Sentences
And Now This
Every Leaf
Barn Tarot

Nonfiction:
Guidebook for Working with Small Independent Publishers